3.74
Sm 4/02
Qw

RUGBY TRIP STORIES

RUGBY TRIP STORIES

David Jandrell and Matthew Tucker

y Lolfa

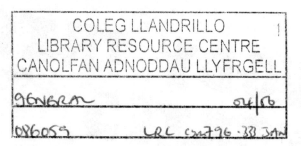
Copyright © David Jandrell, Matthew Tucker & Y Lolfa Cyf. 2006

Illustrations: Sion Jones

ISBN: 0 86243 871 3

Printed on acid-free and partly recycled paper
and published and bound in Wales by
Y Lolfa Cyf., Talybont, Ceredigion SY24 5AP
e-mail ylolfa@ylolfa.com
website www.ylolfa.com
tel (01970) 832 304
fax 832 782

The Fans

Introduction

So, Christmas is over. New Year is over. Phew! Let's get back to normality and give the body a well-deserved rest from excessive boozing and general over-indulgence.

What's next? Easter? Better lose a few pounds because there'll be lots of chocolate to get through when Easter arrives!

But wait! What about the rugby? Forgot about that! Better prepare the body for another massive influx of the 'runny stuff'. Never mind, can't ignore the rugby can we? I mean, it's the Six Nations Tournament! A mammoth struggle which is watched worldwide, and other places as well.

Hundreds of thousands of fans flock to grounds and cram themselves into pubs to watch huge, fit, hard, vicious, aggressive, non-compromising men battle it on muddy pitches with the sound of National Anthems and other songs ringing in their ears.

What a spectacle!

For some people, the game is not the most important thing. Okay, they'd like their team to win, but even that may not be paramount in their eyes. The main attraction for them is the away trip.

Gone are the days, if they were ever here, when people left the house in time to arrive at the ground just before the kick off and made their way straight home after the final whistle.

The match day is a full day. Up early, huge stodgy breakfast and out on the booze by 10am. Back home after shut tap, so full of beer that you sound like a hot water bottle as you stagger home. Oh, and you catch the game as well.

That's what happens when your team is at home. When they're away… you get four days of it, sometimes even more!

When lots of people come into contact with lots of booze, miles away from home, funny things happen. A great deal of research has gone into these 'funny things' and lots of people have told me about things that have happened on away trips.

As you can imagine, I have been told hundreds of great stories and here are just some of them. There are some even better ones, but these are the only printable ones!

The Start of it All

"Right lads, get changed quickly now and get out on the field. You boy, are you doing games? No? Got a note? Oh, forgot your kit eh? Strip off and do it in your pants then! The rest of you, hurry up and line up by the door in a single file in twos. Oh, and Webb Ellis, no nonsense this week please, or you're in trouble, matey."

That was 1823 – the year, not the time (they probably didn't have 24 hour clocks then) – when the PE teacher at Rugby school gathered together his charges – their brains still frazzled from double chemistry – for a good old game of football, prior to letting them loose on the Latin mistress who had the pleasure of their company until lunchtime.

And, so the story goes, the proud PE teacher strode onto the playing fields at Rugby, closely followed by his band of budding footballers, keen to run off all their pent up aggression and frustration built up over endless hours of academic training in the main school building. Er… except for Webb Ellis, not a fan of PE, or football for that matter. It would be fair to say that young William and his sports teacher didn't exactly see eye-to-eye.

Moving on a bit, the game is in full swing and the lads are keen to do the best for their side, but even more keen to convince the teacher that they have put enough effort into the game to avoid the statutory 'five laps of the pitch followed by twenty press-ups' punishment doled out to those deemed to have 'not been pulling their weight'.

This almost standard method of punishment is surely the reason why I was the World Press-Up Champion of Newbridge Grammar School for three years on the trot.

At a very early stage in my education, I learned that the best way to be able to fulfill the punishment at the end of each PE lesson was to conserve my energy during it – a strategy which served me very well throughout my formative years.

Anyway, back to Rugby school. It was a pretty mundane game, apparently, when suddenly, a great shout was heard:

"Pass the ball to Webb Ellis! Go on son, you're on your own – nobody's marking you! Go for it!"

Young Webb Ellis watched the ball as it sailed through the air towards him. Finally, he was going to do something to make his teacher proud of him. The ball arrived, and Webb Ellis… picked up the ball and ran with it! "What?" I hear you say, "Picked up the ball and ran with it? He's not supposed to do that." The PE teacher was reportedly heard to say something similar.

And that, as the same story goes, was the beginning of Rugby Football. I've never believed a word of it, especially after reading several related articles, where it is well-documented that the tale is a myth, when I was researching for this book.

Nevertheless, since that fateful day, a stone tablet has appeared at Rugby school, bearing the message:

THIS STONE

COMMEMORATES THE EXPLOIT OF

WILLIAM WEBB ELLIS

WHO WITH A FINE DISREGARD FOR THE RULES OF

FOOTBALL

AS PLAYED IN HIS TIME

FIRST TOOK THE BALL IN HIS ARMS AND RAN

WITH IT

THUS ORIGINATING THE DISTINCTIVE FEATURE

OF

THE RUGBY GAME

A.D. 1823

I am also very sceptical about another tale which tells of what happened when the PE teacher finally caught up with Webb Ellis after he 'took the ball in his hands and ran with it'.

This story tells of the way that the schoolmaster took the ball from young Will and inserted it into a place 'where the sun doesn't shine'.

It took so long to extract the ball from its temporary resting place, that it had assumed the now very familiar shape known to all rugby player and fans!

So, the sport of Rugby Football – which has been described as 'the game played by fifteen men with funny shaped balls', 'egg-chasing' (mainly by soccer fans), and the 'gentleman's game' (mainly by rugby fans) – whether we like it or not, it is here to stay.

Most people in Wales do like it, and it was with great pride and pleasure that we accepted the accolade of Triple Crown, Six Nations Champions and Grand Slam winners of 2005.

This surprised a lot of people – mainly us – when in early spring 2005 we were to be facing Ireland at the Millennium Stadium with the BIG THREE titles up for grabs.

We only went and won it, didn't we!

All the other nations seemed chuffed to beans as well. Why, it was only Mr Dallaglio himself who said that "Wales could lose every other match in the series, then beat England and consider it to have been a successful season."

I'm not altogether sure that this is completely accurate. I was always under the impression that all rugby nations thought that – not just Wales. I have spoken to people who support other teams and they all say the same things. Mind you, I've only spoken to some French, Scots, Irish, Italians, Kiwis, South Africans, Aussies …er …Romanians, Argentine-ans, Fijians, Japanese, Western Samoans and even someone from the whole of Samoa.

But enough of that, it's time to move on to the history of the game.

Or is it? The history of the game has been dealt with so many times before. It isn't going to change; why revisit it again here?

Apart from… D.U.F.C. …otherwise known as Trinity College Rugby Club, of the University of Dublin, Dublin, Ireland… Est. 1834, claimed to be the oldest club in the world. What I want to know is… in their early days, who did they play?

And another thing, I notice that there are just as many references claiming that the William Webb Ellis incident *did* herald the beginnings of the modern game as there are that claim it didn't.

Did it? Didn't it?

This is not the place to debate this point, but there must be someone out there who knows the truth. If you are that person, please let us know.

Now is the time to move on to the subject of this book – the fans and trips that they go on in pursuit of watching their team.

Fans

Supporters of the 'football' genre of ball games usually fall into two categories: those who follow the 'round ball' game, and those who follow the 'oval ball' game.

There has always been a lot of discussion between both sets of fans, each proclaiming their preferred game as being the better of the two.

Most of the banter is concerned with the skill levels and fitness levels of the players. Soccer stalwarts have always maintained that players of their game are far more talented and fitter than rugby players, comparing players such as Giggs, Ronaldinho and the like with stereotypical lumbering rugby forwards. Since the introduction of professionalism, the gap between the fitness levels of these sets of players has been closing rapidly.

Another area which has caused conflict is concerned with the violence associated with soccer crowds. Whilst it has become less common these days, rugby fans are always quick

to point out that opposing supporters mingle on the terraces and enjoy the spirit of the game together.

The soccer boys counter this move with: "Aye, alright – there is a bit of that going on, but in rugby all the violence is happening on the pitch!"

As far as the rugby fans are concerned, there are mainly two types: those who support the game, and those who go to internationals.

The bloke who stands in all weathers – usually with half a dozen others – and who watches his local team week in and week out, has to watch the international games on TV.

Gone are the days when Joe Public could just buy a ticket and go to an international.

I can remember being taken to my first international in the early sixties at Cardiff Arms Park and thinking, "Hmmm, this is alright this is, I think I'll come to some more of these."

The trouble is, tickets were quite hard to come by even in those days, so a few more years went by before I went again – with some of the lads. They had been going for years!

Where had they got their tickets from? "Tickets!! You don't need tickets to get in there mun!" was the reply.

In those days, people queued for miles to get in, and all you did was join a queue and wait until you finally got to the turnstile. Those without tickets simply put cash on the counter, usually ten bob, and the turnstile made the familiar 'clank' sound which meant you were in! I mean, if you were at the turnstile, they couldn't turn you back, as the queues behind you were so great, it was impossible to get back out.

Another method that worked was to spend ages rummaging through pockets, wallets and any other place where a ticket could hide, occasionally glancing at the turnstile operator and saying, "It's here somewhere, mate," before continuing to rummage. It doesn't take many of those, coupled with shouts of "C'mon, hurry up mun!" from those in the queue behind, for the turnstile operator to get fed up and let you in.

It is not possible, as far as I know, to get into games in this way any more – particularly with grounds being all-seaters, you've got nowhere to go if you're in there by illicit means. No, I'm afraid you just must have a ticket.

Nowadays, the demand for tickets is even more frantic and has become big business.

It has become popular to use international matches as corporate jollies, where companies organise a day out for their most valued customers, which includes top nosh and a ticket for the game.

So how do companies end up with all the tickets and why can't fans buy tickets over the counter? This is all about sponsorship.

Local companies sponsor small club sides and receive, in return, company logos and ads in programmes, placards placed along the perimeter of the field, and the clubs' allocation of tickets. Armed with a plethora of tickets, businesses can impress clients on match days.

Companies will hire venues near the ground and meet and greet their customers and chaperone them to the venue where they will be treated to free booze and two free meals (pre-match and post-match) before being given some of the best seats in the ground. The fact that many of these people have little knowledge or understanding of the game is by the by – it's just a nice day out, isn't it? A chance to talk shop with someone you've spoken to thirty times a day for the last ten years on the telephone, yet never met.

WOAT's

At one match, I had the misfortune of sitting behind someone who was obviously on a jolly in the Millennium Stadium. The game had progressed until half-time, when – as the whistle went and the teams were walking off for a cuppa – she turned to her husband and in a very posh voice asked, "So which are Wales, then?"

There were some very big clues there that had appeared to have passed her by.

- As she was in Wales, she may have realised that great shouts of encouragement boomed around the ground every time someone in red got the ball.

- As Wales were playing the All Blacks, the colours that one of the teams was wearing was a bit of a giveaway.

The husband explained which team was which, and she responded with "So Wales are the team in red and the All Blacks are the ones in black… Er, is that why they call them the All Blacks?"

A new word has emerged in recent years; I don't know its origin or whether it has made it into the dictionary yet – the word is WOAT. It is an acronym for 'Waste of a Ticket'. In some cases I believe that WOAT is an apt word to use, particularly in the case of the "Is that why they call them the All Blacks?" woman.

While I was conducting my research in a pub prior to the same game, I was interested when I became aware of a conversation between a female Wales supporter and a male supporter who 'talked funny':

"You d'talk funny, where are you from then?"

"New Zealand."

"Aw, there's lovely, on 'oliday are you?"

"No, I've come to watch the rugby."

"Oooh, you'll love it! It'll be a lovely experience for you to take back with you. Never been before, have you?"

"Oh, I've been lots of times."

"Well fancy! Funny though really, innit, seeing as you haven't got a team, like. Pity innit."

"What do you mean 'we haven't got a team'?"

"Well you haven't, have you? Got a team like?"

"Yes, we have a team."

"Have you? Any good?"

By this time, the New Zealander had realised that she was not trying to be offensive, and thought that by the time the conversation had reached the "Have you? Any good?" stage, it was time to go and stand somewhere else.

Our heroine was then surrounded by her mates, who let her into a little secret. This was followed with a shriek, which was in turn followed with a "Oh my God! I didn't know the All Blacks was from New Zealand!"

This outburst was loud enough for the New Zealander to hear, and the smile on his face was nearly wide enough to stop the traffic in St Mary Street.

Well, she promised him 'a lovely experience to take back', and came through with the goods. I wonder how many times that story has been told around the pubs in Kiwiland?

Another story tells of a colleague who was allocated a customer to meet and look after for the day at an international – this time in the old National Stadium.

My colleague, who wishes to remain anonymous, but whose real name is Stuart Walker, met the gent at Cardiff

General Station at around midday and started to lead him towards the venue that the company had hired for the day.

Stuart suspected that something was amiss when the customer said, "I hear you have a very good museum in Cardiff, is it near here?"

After a look around the museum, the castle and a few book shops he asked Stuart if there would be enough time to buy some presents for the wife and kids after the game, or would it be best to do it before. They did it before!

They got into the ground with about two minutes to spare before the kick-off , armed with carrier bags full of 'Welshy' souvenirs – not the place to visit with your shopping.

During the game, the visitor flicked through some books that he had bought and told Stuart how much he was going to enjoy reading them on the train home!

When the final whistle went, Stuart was confident that he'd get his 'customer' into the company do for some grub and a few pints, but wait! The customer had spotted a nice little restaurant in town that he liked the look of. Could they go there instead?

They dined at the 'nice little restaurant'. Stuart picked up the tab out of his own pocket!

And then it happened! The customer thought it would be nice to have a drink before catching his train home. Stuart almost manhandled him into the Royal Hotel (which was the nearest hostelry at the time), and marvelled at the look on his companion's face when he saw, for the first time, the interior of a Cardiff bar after a game! 'They were swinging off the chandeliers' was one term Stuart used when he described the 'goings on'.

He was brought back down to earth, when our visitor

requested "A dry sherry if I may," when asked what he wanted to drink.

Now that is a WOAT!

Anyway, enough of WOATs – let's examine the adventures of those who actually take the trips to watch the big games – the travelling supporters.

Travels

Supporters who intend to see every game in a six nations tournament will be facing at least two away games, which may both be overseas! A very daunting prospect, you may think, and something which may be a bit of a bind. Quite the opposite! Away matches are to be relished, saved for and planned for anything up to two years.

Wherever fans are heading, there is usually a bus involved. The bus may be taking fans directly to the ground or it may be taking them to meet other forms of transport – ferries, trains, planes etc.

Buses are hives of activity where antics are concerned. One in particular sticks out in my mind. When I spoke about planning earlier, this is a classic example of forward planning and precision timing when put into operation.

This involves the purchase of a tin of vegetable soup prior to boarding the bus. The variety with the thick lumps usually works the best.

The target will be 'tour virgins' – those who are on their first trip.

The activity involves a seasoned campaigner, a veteran of several years of travelling away, announcing to the rest of the bus that he feels sick. This usually happens about twenty minutes into the journey. The 'sickie' will then proceed to make 'being sick' noises, loud enough to be heard by everyone on the bus. When he has finished, he will walk to the front of the bus, armed with a clear plastic bag filled with the vegetable soup, supposedly about to deposit the bag into the waste bin at the front of the bus.

As he nears the waste bin, a collaborator (another seasoned campaigner who will have positioned himself amongst a group of 'tour virgins') will plead with the 'sickie' to sell him the bag and its contents as he missed his breakfast and is starving. After a paltry sum and the 'bag of soup' have changed hands, the collaborator will miraculously produce a spoon from his pocket and begin to eat the contents of the bag in front of the horrified tour virgins.

I have seen this trick performed three times and reactions have been mixed. Sure, horror is usually the initial reaction to this ritual, but on one occasion it was met with another bout of sickness from one of the people who was witnessing it for the first time – this time for real. The situation was quickly diffused, however, when the driver, who had obviously seen it several times before, announced over the in-bus intercom, "When you've finished that, butt, there's another lot over by here for you."

Yes, unfortunately, these tour virgins get the brunt of most of the pranks that are used on these trips.

Another favourite is the passport prank.

As the Six Nations tournament involves travelling to other countries, passports will be needed to enter overseas countries. There will however always be one person – generally a UK-based tour virgin – who will believe that a passport is necessary to travel to one of the other countries within the UK.

Of course, the rookie will not be informed that a passport

is required until well into the journey! Usually it will be the trip leader who will make an announcement to the occupants of the bus, which will be something like "Make sure that your passports are ready when we get to the Severn Bridge, we don't want to get held up there again, like last year, do we?"

It won't be long before the rookie will make contact with the trip leader and inform him that he hasn't got a passport. This will lead to a panic that will involve all the passengers who will offer solutions to the problem. Once it has been decided that they cannot turn back to get the passport, the only option will be to 'smuggle' the rookie into the country.

I have heard reports of people spending return journeys in luggage racks and under seats for fear of being charged with being illegal immigrants.

Trains can also be used for this scam, and I must say that it is much more comfortable to spend eight hours in a train toilet than lying in the back of a transit van with everybody else's luggage on top of you.

Needless to say, people who have fallen for this trick will never be subjected to any ridicule when they get home. The old saying, 'What happens on tour stays on tour,' will be honoured and the secret of the passport checkpoint dodger will never be mentioned in the village or local rugby club. And if you believe that…

One of my favourite 'rookie quests' was that of the £100 prize offered to those who could catch a live haggis from the countryside around the hotel where some fans were staying prior to a Wales v Scotland match a number years ago.

On the way up to Scotland, the rookies were told of a mythical Scottish beast which roams the Scottish moors – the Haggis. So the story goes, there used to be millions of these

haggises roaming Scotland until the Scots found out they tasted nice, and then they were hunted to near extinction. Nowadays, haggises are raised in battery farms, but to find a wild one is very unusual. The princely sum of one hundred pounds would be given to the first person to capture a live haggis and bring it back to the hotel – its fate: to sit in a glass case on the bar at the rugby club back home.

The haggis was described as an ugly looking beast, about the size and shape of a marrow. It was covered in fur of various colours, resembling tartan, which, by the way, is why the Scots started wearing tartan in the first place.

The best way to catch a haggis is to crawl around in the undergrowth whilst making the sound that the haggis is attracted to. The sound? You've guessed it… the sound of the bagpipes.

I built a mental picture of the tale as it was related to me, of the scene from the hotel window when the rest of the tour party watched with glee as three rookies hunted for the elusive beast in the fields next to the hotel car park.

It is quite a similar trick to that played on some French visitors, who after sampling faggots, peas and chips at a local chippy, spent a morning looking for faggots in the Welsh countryside, after rather foolishly asking what they were.

I don't know whether the scam was spurred by the haggis-hunting or if it was a touch of off-the-cuff genius by the perpetrator, but nevertheless they fell for it.

They were particularly intrigued by the description of these faggots – 'about the size of snooker balls, covered in long hair. They roll around the countryside at speeds exceeding 100mph and emit a loud high-pitched squeaking sound. You have to be very fast to catch them – it's best to trap them in a corner and throw a towel over them.'

Armed with a few towels, the Frenchmen strode off into the countryside and returned four hours later disappointed and faggotless!

Next time we play the USA, I hope that someone doesn't play that trick on any American fans. The term 'faggot-hunting' has a totally different meaning to them!

Rules for the trip

All trips will have a leader, usually a senior member of the rugby club, who may be involved in some sort of managerial position at his workplace.

He'll organise the bus, make sure everyone is aware of all the arrangements *before* setting off and attempt, usually unsuccessfully, to maintain order throughout the duration of the trip.

In order to do this, ground rules have to be laid down to give people some idea of the sort of behaviour that is expected of them.

A typical set of guidelines would resemble these.

- People must present themselves at the bar by 10am at the latest, and be in possession of a full pint. This is *every* morning.

- All members of the party must wear, at all times, the predetermined 'dress' that will have been deemed compulsory before embarking on the trip.

- All members of the party must carry, at all times, the predetermined item that will have been deemed compulsory before embarking on the trip.

- The "Eatin' is Cheatin" rule must be adhered to at all times. Eating after a skinful is acceptable and should only consist of various fast foods such as kebabs, curries, chips etc. Eating prior to long bouts of drinking is taboo on the basis that it's bad for you to 'eat on an empty stomach'.

- Hotel key fobs must be carried at all times. Sometimes this is the only means of getting back to hotels. If you are in such a state of inebriation that you can't speak, the art of waving your key fob at a taxi driver is certain to get you back safely.

This list is by no means inexhaustible and will vary from club to club – but I think you get the idea.

There are those who will fall foul of these rules and will have to make an appearance in front of a Kangaroo Court in order to answer all charges. A Kangaroo Court will consist of… well… the entire tour party, from which a chairman, jury, prosecution and defence lawyers will be selected. The defence lawyers will, of course, be of no assistance to the defendant, and will, in fact, do more harm than good during the trial.

And so the trial will begin. The charges will be read out and the prosecuting 'lawyer' will put his case forward. The defence 'lawyer' will add his bit which will contain even more incriminating evidence than the prosecutor could muster. Throughout the proceedings, the 'crowd' will jeer and boo, just to make the defendant feel that he has the full support of them all.

Then the jury will be asked to consider the verdict, before declaring the defendant guilty.

Once the inevitable 'guilty' verdict has been found, the chairman will decide the grisly fate of the defendant.

This will involve the guilty party having to indulge in some form of activity that will be

- Disgusting
- Dangerous
- Vulgar
- Distasteful

or all of these. Whatever the sentence, it will be something that you will never want your wife, girlfriend (or either, for that matter), family, boss or even the police to find out about.

Standard penalties are

- Bolting (drinking down in one) pints. The number of pints to be bolted and the contents of the pint glasses will vary according to the gravity of the offence.

- Spending the rest of the trip in some kind of fancy dress.

- Waiting on people, maybe the hierarchy of the club, but almost always, the chairman, who will be the one who has dished out the sentence. The person who is to be waited upon, may decide that this must be done in some form of fancy dress, and will make sure that there will be several instances of this having to be done in public.

- Eating things that will bring tears to your eyes – cat food sandwiches, leftovers in restaurants etc.

The best advice to give to would-be rugby trippers, is to find out if your club operates a Kangaroo Court system of discipline and if they do, go with someone else. If your club confirms to you that they do not operate Kangaroo Courts, don't believe them and go with someone else.

Make sure that the 'someone else' you are going to go with don't operate kangaroo Courts, and if they say they don't, don't believe them.

Just to be on the safe side, go on your own.

Memorabilia

One of the main aims of going on trips is to bring something back to remind you of the occasion. On the whole, the art of collecting memorabilia is more commonly known as 'nicking stuff'. In fact, buying something is not really as highly re-garded as pinching something – well, pinched stuff is free, for a start!

What kinds of thing get stolen in the pursuit of memo-rabilia? Well, anything that is of little use to the 'pincher' really. And if you've heard the saying 'nothing's safe unless it's screwed down', don't fret, these boys take screwdrivers round with them!

Let's see: signs are quite popular. Particularly popular are those that indicate the way to somewhere that the trip is heading – a sign saying "Lansdowne Road next left" would be a perfect trophy to be hung in the bar at the local rugby club for example.

Probably the most high profile sign that made its way to Wales was one saying "Wembley Stadium", and it came back in a Volkswagon Beetle.

Getting that into a Beetle was an artform in itself. It was strategically placed in the gap between driver's and passenger's seat. It was touching the windscreen, the roof and the back window. It formed a perfect partition, cutting the interior of the car in half to such an extent that the driver couldn't see the passenger and the two people in the back couldn't see each other either! It must have been a very uncomfortable journey home.

It was even more uncomfortable when at about 3am, the vehicle reached the toll at the Severn Bridge. The occupants had decided to do the driving in shifts – the last shift was from the Severn Bridge home. As the vehicle stopped, the driver and front seat passenger swapped positions for the final leg of the journey. The trouble was, the new driver, who was a bit stewed after having been asleep for a few hours, failed to restart the vehicle. After stalling it a few times, the occupants of the little police control room near the toll booths came out to see what the trouble was. After checking with the driver, and checking the vehicle – the only one that was on the road at that time, they were happy to give the car a 'shove' for a few yards enabling the driver to bump start it. They were off, and to show their appreciation, gave the helpful bobbies a cheeky little 'toot' to thank them for their troubles. But mainly in relief that not one of the four policemen had noticed a sign of that magnitude, bearing the words 'Wembley Stadium' which effectively split the car in half along its length.

That is probably one of the most extreme 'sign nicks' that came to light as a result of researching this book.

Another involved the theft of a 10ft banner. This was spotted on a building in Ireland and was immediately targeted as a worthwhile trophy. The trouble was, it was draped 50ft high on the front of the building! The precarious position that the banner occupied and all the dangers that were associated with acquiring it were completely outweighed by the desire to own it. Needless to say, some intrepid tourists managed to scale the building and remove it without too much difficulty. But what to do with it?

It seemed to be obvious – place it over the chairman's bed back at the hotel, particularly as the banner read 'The Chairman is Coming'.

Apparently, the chairman didn't like it!

Menu boards are also quite sought after, as are pub signs, street signs and, well anything that will cause shock and horror when they're the first things that perpetrators see when they wake up in dingy hotel rooms.

"Oh my God, what's that hanging on the wardrobe? Not the revolving 'NEW SCOTLAND YARD' sign that you see on the news, is it?"

A quick blink and a swift rubbing of eyes, followed by a tentative peep in the direction of the wardrobe, will confirm that it is in fact the sign in question. Then a groan, as the activities of the previous night slowly come flooding into the room.

One of the most unusual 'nicks' is that of a tramp's coat. It has come to my attention that a group of 'lads on a trip' were walking around a large English city in search of a suitable watering hole, when they passed a tramp who was having a breather in a shop doorway. He had placed all his belongings in a tidy pile and draped his coat neatly over the top of them, presumably to minimize the chances of getting creases in it.

As the group turned a corner and headed in another direction, it became apparent that the guy bringing up the rear of the entourage had something different about him. He was wearing a coat – a tramp's coat. In fact it was *the* tramp's coat, you know, the one they'd just passed!

Luckily enough, the new occupier of the coat found something in one of the pockets. It was a packet of chewing gum. He offered them around but didn't get any takers, so he ate them himself. Great, innit? Well, waste not, want not, as the saying goes.

Sometimes, when large sporting events are held in a big city, a carnival atmosphere descends upon the whole place. Many places have city centre fairgrounds with jugglers, merry-go-rounds and little motorbikes that take 50p pieces and chug around little circuits that are enclosed by wooden boxes. These little motorbikes do about 200 yards per 50p, but when riders are continually going round and round, it seems like they go for miles.

Now what if someone with a pocketful of 50p's arranged for one of the retaining 'boxes' to be moved sufficiently to allow the width of a bike to 'escape', and with an accomplice to drive whilst he continually pumped 50p's into the slot on the bike, how far do you think they'd get? Well, farther than you'd think, particularly if you actually make it onto the main road before the 'ride owners' can catch up with you!

"Nobody did this though?" I hear you say.

"Oh yes, they did!"

Expecting an urgent call? Left your mobile back at the hotel? Whatever can you do? Why not pinch a payphone from one of the pubs that you've been drinking in all night?

An excellent idea! And so it came to pass that one hapless person found himself in the unenviable position of being extremely well-oiled, cold, lost and standing outside a pub in possession of a payphone. Is there anything worse than that? Oh aye!

Added to our hero's already horrendous predicament was the sight of two policemen with dogs approaching him at great speed. 'Teeth like daggers' I think was the term he used when describing the scene coming at him. Apparently the dogs' teeth were even worse!

To be fair, one of the officers gave him an opportunity to escape. The terms of the agreement was that they'd give him two minutes to leg it before letting the dogs off their leads, or he just got into the van without a fuss. After a short period of consideration, he got into the van without a fuss. Chicken!

Presents

Hotels can provide good presents to take back home to those who have allowed you to engage in a weekend of joviality and debauchery. To be honest, a rugby trip does not create

the best environment to browse around the shops in search of gifts for the wife and kids. Instead, it may be necessary to search the hotel for trinkets, and what better place to start than your room? Rooms contain lots of complementary stuff provided by the hotel management and that rarely get used – soap, shampoo, chocs, Gideon Bibles, sachets of salt, pepper, vinegar, towels, bedding, trouser presses… *trouser presses?* According to those that have managed it, the best strategy to adopt if you are going to remove items as substantial as these is to make sure your room is virtually intact, lock it and remove the item you want from someone else's room: preferably someone who is not on your trip. Even more preferably, someone who is not connected with rugby at all.

That way, the good name of people who go on rugby trips will not be tarnished in any way. We wouldn't want that, would we?

The Match Day

Whether you are a home supporter or a visitor, you will need to spend a bit of time in the city that contains the ground that will host your team.

You will be within arm's length of all the cultural activities and venues that each city has to offer, and many people take the opportunity to participate in these pursuits during their trip. Many more people don't.

Regardless of the plethora of museums, art galleries, areas of natural beauty, cathedrals etc., that are contained within these cities, they are generally not inundated with fans prior to and after each game. So where do they go?

A study was carried out, in Cardiff, to find out exactly what 'goes on' on match days. The findings, gathered from years of experience of attending matches and participating in the most popular activities, are detailed below.

Research has shown that most rugby fans would prefer to have a few pints before the game – and after the game, a few more.

Further research has also shown that partaking of a few during the game is also fairly popular. Some more in-depth, personal research, taken during the 2005 Autumn Internationals at the Millennium Stadium, has revealed that five pints during the game is just about feasible. Seven is pushing it – particularly when you bear in mind the 'waiting at the bar' time, the 'travelling time' from your seat to the bar and back and the 'travelling time' from your seat to the toilets. You should also try to catch a piece of the game during this onslaught.

If you are going to have a go at a seven-pinter, you should also make sure that you have an aisle seat – not that it will cut much time off your journeys, but it will cut down the amount of abuse that you will suffer from the people who share your row as you are continually asking them to stand up for you to get out. After about four of these sojourns, you will begin to receive additional abuse from those who are occupying seats in the row behind yours.

It is important to add that half-time is probably the worst time to visit toilets and re-fill glasses as this is the period that is most popular with the rest of the crowd who wish to do these things. Trying to perform these duties at half-time could take three pints off the feasible amount that can be consumed during the game, as queues for both facilities are absolutely horrendous! Perhaps there is a case for the rugby authorities to consider extending this aspect of the game to at least half an hour. In other words, 'going for it' must be done with half-time taken completely out of the equation.

So, people who actually take up the 'seven pint challenge', must make sure that they've arranged for someone to record the match so that they can actually see it when they get home, even though they've been to the game.

The travelling times to and from the bar and to and from toilets does take a substantial chunk out of the time available to watch the match.

When you take into account that all drinks consumed during the game are over and above those taken during the pre- and post-match festivities, some people may find difficulty in comprehending exactly what is happening on the pitch. Research has shown that in the most extreme cases, some people have been unaware of the result of matches they've been to by the time they get home. It is quite a common practice for people to be misled as to the actual result of matches on their return to local pubs and rugby clubs, when 'friends' who have stayed at home and watched the game on TV realise that they are in such a state of inebriation that they will believe just about anything. These people have also be informed that the TV cameras were on them at least half a dozen times throughout the game and these friends will describe in detail 'what you were doing' at the time and witnessed by countless millions of people all over the world who were enjoying the match on TV.

These reports will include incidents such as

- Being spotted having a fag, when you have sworn to 'never touch another one', made worse by the fact that you said you'd pay a fiver to anyone who spots you doing so. Everyone in the club will have seen this and be queuing up for payment.

- Exposing yourself live on telly.

- You were seen fraternizing with a young lady, usually extremely attractive, who was sitting directly behind you.

- You were also seen fraternizing with an older lady, usually extremely unattractive, who was sitting in the seat in front of you.

- After the game, when a prominent seventies ex-player was being interviewed in Westgate Street, you were clearly seen, in the background, urinating into a waste bin.

Of course, when the game is actually viewed on video, the victim will become aware that the team that had reportedly won hadn't, and that he had never once featured in live TV close-ups as alleged in the club the night before.

In many cases, and personal research confirms this, watching the game on a Sunday is just about the only activity that can be carried out following international days.

I have found that the best way to cope with post-international hangovers is to put off the 'getting up' process to as late as possible, before staggering to the settee and staying there for the rest of the day. For some, not prone to hangovers, a 'quiet' Sunday is enough to recuperate and make it to work on Monday feeling one hundred percent and fully refreshed. For others, and I am one of these, the hundred percent and fully-refreshed feeling does not arrive until the following Tuesday.

Apart from the drinking, it is compulsory to make a visit to Caroline Street. Caroline Street is a stagger and a half away from the ground and no visit to Cardiff is complete without sampling the wares in what is known to many as 'the street of a thousand chip shops' and to the rest, 'Chip Alley'.

It seems that everyone who has attended matches at the National Stadium or the Millennium Stadium makes a beeline for Caroline Street straight after the final whistle. I know I always have. There is no sight like it. Hundreds of people milling about, eyes fixed on one thing: take-away chicken curry off-the-bone and chips, pasty and chips, fish and chips, sausage in batter and chips, kebab and chips, all wrapped in yesterday's *Echo*.

People with vinegar running up their arms, whilst trying to clutch their prized meal as close to their bodies as possible, in an attempt to stop it from being crushed into a pulp by the heaving crowds. But do they care? Not a chance.

Then there's the glorious Clark's Pie! Are there enough superlatives in our language to describe the Clark's Pie? I doubt it. If they're not world-famous, they blinkin' well ought to be.

Unfairly, Caroline Street has probably been cited as the cause of hundreds of post-match hangovers, as flagging match-goers lie groaning on the settee the next day.

"Feeling a bit rough today are you luv?"

"Oh aye, suffering a bit to be honest."

"Went down Caroline Street again did you?"

"Aye, well all the boys wanted grub see."

"Well, you didn't have to go, you know it always makes you bad."

"Gotta show willin', haven't you?"

"I got no sympathy with you."

"Must've put too much vinegar on my chips, I expect."

"I'll cut you some sandwiches for the next game – save you going down there, innit."

"Aye, that'll be a good idea."

Strangely enough, the sixteen pints and double vodka chasers consumed throughout the day, never seemed to be mentioned as contributory factors in feeling a bit dicky the day after a match!

The majority of people are resigned to watching the game on TV. The three venues that are most popularly used for this are: home, the pavement outside electrical stores where you can watch the game on 79 sets simultaneously whilst out shopping, or the pub.

Many people take the trek to Cardiff just to watch the game in the city pubs, and take in the 'atmosphere'. I have known people who have attended the pre-match festivities in Cardiff pubs and chosen to stay there throughout the game, even though they have tickets to go into the ground! Well, it's one way of making sure you have a seat when the massive influx of those who have gone to the game arrive for the post-match sesh!

Local pubs are generally the most popular for those who are inclined to watch the rugby on TV but don't take the trip to Cardiff, and landlords usually 'push the boat out' when it comes to match day.

Placards strategically placed around the exterior of these establishments herald the oncoming match and inform potential clientele of the free half-time tempters.

On offer will be the statutory 'big screen' which can only be viewed successfully if the viewer is right in front of it, 'goodies' on the bar, which will consist of plastic bowls full of salted peanuts and a free meal at half-time.

This will usually be chicken curry and chips, but some pubs offer sausage and chips, corned beef pie and chips or whatever else is on offer at the Cash and Carry with chips.

Whatever the offer, pubs are packed out on match days with people sporting their teams' colours and ready to engage in the festivities and banter of the games.

The majority of punters will be supporting their country, but there will always be one or two people that will be 'shouting for' the other side. Every village will have at least one ex-pat from one of the other six nations and they will be quick to pull on their teams' colours and head to the pub to cheer them on. These are normally well tolerated and healthy banter is a common feature of the friendly rivalry associated with these occasions.

The worst punters are the neutrals, who always seem to shout for the team that is playing the team that the rest of the punters are supporting.

"I honestly don't care who wins. I just hope your lot loses. It's not that I don't like your lot, I just think the others are better."

Of course, these cheer the loudest when their 'adopted' preferred side scores and scoff at any score that the 'home' side manages.

"That was never a try! He was offside for a start, and it was a forward pass. He knocked it on, put his foot in touch before he went over, and he didn't even ground the ball properly!"

These are very popular snubs designed to wind up the rest of the pub. They work, of course. Whilst people like this are generally despised by pub rugby watchers, they are rarely faced with violence. Instead, the revenge is usually much more subtle. Of course they will be subject to copious quantities of verbal abuse, which is what they are trying to encourage.

Let's just say that people who set out to 'create waves' in this environment should be advised, if they have any belongings with them, to take everything into the toilet with them when they have to 'make a visit', including their pints. Oh, and be sure to check their seat before sitting down when they return. I'll enlarge on this no further.

The Six Nations Trips

IRELAND

If you are one of these people who enjoys travelling in
comfort on those smooth journeys, then cross your name off
the Ireland trip: whether travelling by air or sea, one thing is
certain – whatever the weather conditions are, you're guaran-
teed a bumpy ride.

By far the best option for travelling to Ireland is to take an
aeroplane. The journey takes about an hour. Take a minute
to glance around the plane before you take your seat just to
see who is sharing the journey with you. If you are lucky,
you could be on the same flight as the players, and a few
ex-legends – usually Gareth Edwards or Phil Bennett – can be
found on these flights.

It is always advisable to cross the Irish Sea during February
or March. The journey takes three hours by cat, or double if
by dinghy. The 'Hewey' (explanation not necessary) crossing
is entertainment in itself, watching the weak-bellied traveller
making the effort to get to the toilet, using a tried-and-tested
method of running full pelt with one hand over the mouth
and the other arm outstretched in order to inform those in the
sufferer's path of 'what is about to happen'.

This method is also very successful as a means to get to the
bar. I have seen four-deep queues at bars disperse very quickly
when they become aware that someone is approaching at great

speed using this pose. They are in for a 'bit of stick' though when they revert to a normal stance and calmly order a round!

One party member was suffering similarly during one of these trips: his colour had changed somewhat from a glowing, healthy look to a kind of olive green. Of course, he received great sympathy and staunch support from fellow travellers as they pretended to be sick by making associated noises and actions. Finally it all got too much for him and he made a quick exit to the loo. The ship's erratic movement was difficult enough to contend with, but when an elderly lady stepped in his path slowing him down even more, he was sure that he was never going to get there. Nevertheless, he did manage it. Sadly, every sink and loo was occupied by people in similar predicaments. Then he saw it! One of the loo doors was ajar. He saw his chance and burst in. He was beyond the point of no return, and even though he was aware that someone was actually sitting on the throne, he was powerless to stop the bewildered tourist wearing the contents of his stomach for the rest of the journey.

If there is a moral to this story, it must surely be 'always lock the door before you sit down.'

Another incident tells of a particularly queasy tourist who was being ill over the side of a ship. Strutting down the deck towards him was another tourist who was feeling no ill effects at all. He was so proud of this fact that he decided to make everyone on the trip know it as well. After a few laps of the deck, he plonked himself next to the lad who was now weak from retching, gulped in a few large breaths of air before announcing;

"Aaah, just experience the fresh sea air. Marvellous innit?"

The lad who was being sick, just glanced at the smug

tourist before continuing to hang over the side of the ship. Keen to rub in how 'hard' he was, the non-suffering tourist added, "Cor, you've got a weak stomach haven't you?"

To which our sick hero replied; "Dunno about that mate, it's chucking it farther than anyone else's."

Needless to say, the Irish have to make the same trip when they come to Wales.

I have heard of a story that I have no reason to believe is true. In fact I can almost guarantee that it isn't – but it's a good 'un anyway.

A travel agent's in Ireland advertised a cheap and nasty trip to Wales for a fiver! As all the other trips were fully booked, one fan decided to take the 'fiver' option.

When he arrived at the jetty, he was shown to an inflatable dinghy and introduced to three other blokes who were going to be his 'travel mates'.

It soon dawned on him that the trip actually involved the four men *rowing* across, and they began to decide on the 'shifts' that they were going to row in for the duration of the trip.

"Well," said the disappointed tourist, "this is a complete rip off. I know it was only a fiver, but to expect us to row across is absolutely ridiculous!"

One of his 'crewmates' replied, "I know, it was the same two years ago an' all!"

Temple Bar

To experience true Ireland, stay clear of Temple Bar.

Temple Bar is an area of Dublin which is akin to St. Mary Street on international match days. So if you want to take in a bit of Irish culture, Temple Bar is not the place to go. If, on the other hand, you've only been in Ireland for a couple of days and you're a bit homesick, then Temple Bar *is* the place to be.

When I said that Temple bar is like St. Mary Street, that's exactly what I meant – everyone there is Welsh, most of them from the valleys, and everyone will know everyone else. I reckon they ought to rename the place "Hiya Butt Street", if not permanently, certainly when Wales are playing in Ireland.

"So where are we going then?"

"Temple Bar."

"Where's that?"

"Here it is, we've just arrived, oh, hiya butt."

"Hiya butt."

"Hiya butt."

"Hiya butt."

"Hiya butt."

"Hiya butt."

Etc.

The atmosphere in Temple Bar is electric, particularly for those who are experiencing it for the first time. Bars flowing with Guinness and everyone supporting their country; Wales, Ireland and whoever England are playing that day.

Guinness Factory

Almost every organised trip to Ireland, includes as part of its itinerary a tour of the Guinness factory. For many, the Guinness trip is the only activity that they get to do over and above the statutory drinking, partying and other associated 'goings on' when visiting the Emerald Isle during the Six Nations period.

I don't know whether the visit would be as well-attended if Guinness produced something other than booze, but it does attract a healthy turnout.

A typical Guinness trip will involve parties of people who are pretending to be interested in the Guinness-making process whilst itching for the invitation at the end to "try some out for yourself."

Yes, the legendary 'free sample' section. Well, you might as well try it out, eh? You've seen how it's made; let's see and taste the outcome.

Firemen on tour

Trips usually involve the compulsory 'wearing of something' which identifies you as being the member of a particular trip. This can be anything from full dress in whatever theme has been dreamed up, to personalised t-shirts with the name of your club or organisation embroidered on front and back, or dummies and other smaller items which nonetheless set you apart from the crowd.

On one particular trip, all tour members went equipped with South Wales Fire Service t-shirts.

They were soon noticed by fellow tourists and became the topic of most conversations.

"So you're firemen, are you?"

"Oh yes, we're all firemen. Doing our duty to those in distress, you know, it's all part of the job…" etcetera.

Once the punters got to know that there was a presence from the South Wales Fire Fighters in the bar, the lads were more or less totally engaged in conversations about the service and the exploits and stories of fire fighting experiences.

The 'fire fighters' were also attracting a lot of female attention as, oddly enough, they had chosen, quite by accident, to imitate servicemen which seem to appeal to the fairer sex much more than any of the others.

A lot of fires were actually extinguished in the bar that night, when, one particularly overzealous 'fire-fighter' announced to the adoring crowd that he was, in fact, the *Chief Constable* of South Wales Fire Service. Time to leave, lads!

A Round for the Girls

Another ploy that did not work exactly to plan was that hatched by a Mr Robert Evans. After many unsuccessful attempts at trying his luck with the ladies, he finally stumbled into a bar which was occupied by a women's rugby team, about 18 girls in all. Bingo! After some light chat he offered to buy a round – 18 women, that's 18 pints of Guinness and a bill of 120 euros… impressive. Now, he can take his pick.

Before some more light chat could take place, the ladies downed their pints and moved on! Aw, not even a kiss, and 120 euros lighter in his pocket. Never mind Robert, you're on tour, these things happen. If you got nothing else from the experience, think of the laugh you have provided us with.

Royalty treatment

Due to the unsavoury nature of some of the 'things' that occur on tour, some people are loathe to divulge their true identities. Others, like Mr Evans of the previous story, are only too happy to claim responsibility for great stories.

Another such person is Mr Matthew Tucker, who has provided us with this gem. These are his own words:

"It has become a regular event for me to dress up in a white 70's suit, with a pink shirt and tie, and a blonde wig during match day. The suit is well-travelled and has been all over the world. This particular story tells of the occasion when a few of my compatriots decided to order a horse and cart to take me to the game.

As I travelled to the ground, a fellow tourist decided to hijack the cart, only to be fended off by the owner, and, after a few hits with his whip I thought it was only fair to tell him that he was a friend and to allow him to stay on. As we made our way down the heaving streets, I positioned myself is such a position where I could blow kisses and issue 'queen waves' to onlookers. I don't know who they thought I was, but they obviously assumed that someone who was making such a grand entrance could only be someone of extreme celebrity status. Maybe the Welsh thought I was an Irish celeb, and the Irish though I was a Welsh celeb. Whichever, I continued to acknowledge the horns, cheers and whistles, which heralded my arrival at our destination – the Jury's Hotel.

It was heaving with supporters and the queue was doubled up for about five hundred yards. We were dropped off at the front of the queue and given a hurried and private entry… perfect! Just as we were about to disappear into our exclusive doorway, I thought it was only fair to turn and greet my followers. I gave the queue a quick wave which was met with an impromptu blast of laughing and cheering. I think they had me sussed, but they seemed to enjoy the moment. Not as much as myself and my side-kick we thought, as we were approaching what was now a nearly completely empty bar manned by eager looking staff who all seemed keen to be the one to serve me.

Missing person!

On one occasion during the Ireland six nations campaign, it had seemed that a tour member had gone missing. After checking his room and other rooms in the hotel, i.e. store room, toilets, kitchen it was decided that he had definitely gone AWOL somewhere. The first thought was that he had probably got lucky and was enjoying himself elsewhere, however, after about 20 Guinness and almost 24 hours had elapsed, suggestions as to the nature of his demise ranged from him being arrested, shot, or tortured. As the party was a particularly caring one, after checking his luggage to see if his clothes would fit any other member of the touring party and if there was any spare cash (beer tokens) lying around, they contacted the police. No luck!

After a further 48 hours – and about six hours before the party was due to leave to travel home – the hotel phone rang. It was him! He told them that he was okay and was in a little place called Shannon with an Irish girl and her family. He informed them that he would not be making the return journey with the rest of the party.

One week later, he returned with his bag on one arm and a little Irish girl on the other.

Travel Kit!

One lucky tourist happened to meet a very attractive 'local' girl and, after getting on really well together, they found themselves in the tourist's hotel room.

The encounter was going quite well and at a crucial stage of the proceedings the question "Have you got a condom?" was posed.

"No, I will go and get one," was the reply.

The tourist made his way to the hotel toilets and addressed the condom machine which was placed in a strategic position on the wall between a mirror and paper towel dispenser.

Our hero looked at the charges and discovered that two euros was the going rate and proceeded to rummage through his pockets in search of some cash.

Luckily enough he had two euros, but that was all he had! He prayed that the machine wouldn't be empty or faulty as he carefully put his entire fortune into the slot.

The money dropped and he quickly yanked on the drawer. Would it open? Yes!! There in all its glory was an open drawer with a little 'parcel' inside it.

Overjoyed, he grabbed his 'parcel' and dashed back to his room. On arrival, he quickly opened his prize to find… a travel kit! Yes, he had a toothbrush, toothpaste, a mirror, some soap. Everything you can think of, except a condom! Ooops!

Willie John McBride

The Welsh have always been well-educated in the rugby world and great names such as Barry John, Gareth Edwards are but a few that have set an example in world rugby. But are we as familiar with 'big names' from other nations? Following yet another defeat at the hands of the Irish, some of the lads sought solace in an Irish pub.

At the bar stood a huge figure of a man with a strong Irish accent. He turned to two of the lads who were buying the round.

Irishman   How you doing Taff?

Welshman   Not too bad, yet another loss, er… you're

	a big 'un. Look at the size of him.
Welshman 2	Did you ever play butt?
Irishman	Um yes, yes once or twice. (*the people around start laughing*)
Welshman	You can tell that.
Welshman 2	Who did you play for?
Irishman	Well I captained Ireland in the 60's and 70's and was captain of the Lions during the seventies.
Both Welshmen	What's your name then?
Irishman	Willie John McBride.
Welshman	Oh, will you sign this then, butt?

Sunday Games

In recent years we have seen the introduction of Sunday games. This is quite popular for TV viewers who get the chance to watch big games live on Saturdays and Sundays, and even the more affluent can travel to two games in a weekend.

It was not popular with fans who travelled to Dublin for an Ireland v Wales game though.

They had planned and saved for two years for this trip, booked tickets and hotels, the Guinness trip, everything.

The trouble was, two years before, they were not aware that the games were to be switched to Sundays. After all the planning and saving every spare penny to put towards the trip, they found that they spent four days in Dublin and travelled back on the day of the match. Blinkin' heck mun!

ITALY

The introduction of Italy into the six nations had a great effect upon the traditional and stereotypical rugby tour, that for years had meant a long weekend away, a well-earned break from the pressure of work and more importantly, the wife.

Suddenly Italy was a part of the great rugby calendar and for loyal rugby fans throughout Wales, a chance to watch your country even deeper into Europe was a delightful thought. Surely the Italians would bring open running rugby and there was, of course, the added bonus... another trip with the boys.

Whilst loyal tourists throughout Wales started to organise the trip to Italy and order their Welsh shirts with the words '*Welsh lads in Italy*' printed around the three feathers, there was something not quite right: the wives were actually *supporting* the trip!

Excitement filled the rugby club as the first Italy tour meeting was arranged for the first Sunday in the Month (another excuse for a hour or two out of the house). As the regular faces sat in the committee room, no-one expected what was to happen next. The door opened and jaws hit the floor as the wives of the husbands sitting around the table announced that it was about time a couples' trip was introduced. Furthermore there was no better place to start the trip than the romantic city itself.

Old campaigners screamed, young campaigners shuddered and single lads fled not only to organise their own trip but also to get away from the hostile atmosphere that suddenly developed in the club.

A new word developed – WOT! No, not WOAT, WOT: an acronym standing for 'Women On Tour', and it has become one of the most feared words in rugby touring circles.

Despite desperate measures to persuade wives to stay at home and even bribing them with the promise of an extra holiday, it was set in stone that Italy would become the trip for husband and wife. Aaah, there's lovely!

So, following two years of organising and nagging, the trip finally arrived. There was something strange about this trip though. It was sort of *different*. Matching luggage replaced the regular kit bag. Pockets usually reserved for cans of beer now contained shoes. Last minute conversations went from "Who's got the beer kitty", "Don't forget the pee bucket", "Just make sure I've got the back seat", "Alright to 'ave a fag on this bus innit?", to; "Have you got the passports?", "Have you got the tickets?", "Have we got the money?", "And I put four pairs of pants and socks in your bag too. Goin' over there for four days with only the ones you've got on is blinkin' ridiculous mun!"

In the end, the lads faced up to the fact that they had to get on with it and for the sake of rugby put on a brave face. They just hoped that come 9pm the women would be tired and go to bed. Then the lads could come out to play.

And did they?

A Visit to a Brothel

Two of the biggest and least 'good-looking' of the lads on the tour decided it would be nice to have one last drink before taking the long walk back to the hotel. They spotted a nice little place that was still open which obviously sold booze.

"Let's have one in here."

"Aye, go on then."

After having been in the bar for about 20 minutes, they became aware that they were getting quite a lot of attention from some really attractive women. This was something that was new to them – they weren't used to uninvited attention from women of *any* description, let alone attractive ones. Not believing their luck, they chatted for ages, bought a few drinks, pinched a few kisses and came to the conclusion that this was one of the best nights they'd ever had.

Until they decided to leave!

The 'great night' suddenly took a turn for the worse. The 'nice little place' that they had spotted was, in fact, a brothel! The owners, *the Mafia*, were not altogether keen on two lads just popping in for a drink and not sampling what the ladies had to offer. They demanded a fee to enable them to leave the premises. This *fee* amounted to £700.

Oddly enough, they didn't have anything like £700 on them and had to surrender all their cash to the Mafia in order to get out. This amounted to somewhere in the region of £200. A small price to pay when you weigh it all up. I can't help wondering what would have happened if they'd decided to be awkward and said, "Seven hundred quid to get out!!! Sod that, we'll stay here."

I have heard of people paying over the odds to get *into* shows and rugby matches, but I think this is the first time I've ever heard of people who have paid to get *out* of a place of entertainment.

Italian Drinking habits

It seems that the Italians have a slightly different view of drinking to that of the common-or-garden rugby tourist. Well, they like a drink, probably the same as most people, it's just the extent of drinking that they come into contact with when visiting supporters go to Rome that they find difficult to come to terms with.

"Why you dreenk so much?" is a phrase commonly heard from Italian bar owners and staff.

Italians seem to drink to quench their thirst, and maybe have a few tipples just to be sociable. They certainly couldn't understand why, in a city like Rome, with all the fantastic sights, art galleries, shops, ancient monuments and fantastic countryside, that people would want to spend four days in a bar, drinking themselves into a stupor, singing songs that didn't make any sense and indulging in practices that are totally alien to the Italian culture.

They didn't seem to be able to realise that drinking is more of a hobby, you know, a way of life. Strange!

Whan Afta?

Language can also create confusion, especially accents. If you go anywhere south and east of France, there seems to be far more scope for misinterpretation of conversations than you would find nearer home. Accents can be even more difficult to decipher when visitors have been 'on the pop', no matter how well locals have mastered English.

I particularly remember two extremely hung-over 'tourists' sitting in a restaurant with the intention of trying to eat something. They didn't really want to, but felt that it made sense to get something inside them that wasn't liquid and didn't contain any alcohol. It might even make them feel better!

The waiter took the orders for the meals and asked the first of our heroes, "You wanna anytheeng to dreenk, sir?"

The very suggestion of 'something to drink' resulted in an act that was most certainly a first for the eyes of the hapless waiter, which could well make it as an Olympic event one day

– Synchronised Heaving!

After a few seconds of frantic swallowing and hot flushes, one of the tourists was able to convey a message to the waiter, "Erm …. I'll have one after."

This was quickly followed by, "I'll have one after as well." from the other poor soul.

The waiter thanked his clients, picked up the menus and strode off into the heart of the restaurant.

Two minutes later, he was back carrying large silver salver on an outstretched arm. Sitting neatly on top of the salver were two of the gaudiest looking drinks that our heroes had ever seen. It was a kind of green colour, with a sort of *shimmer* to it. A bit like antifreeze. It also came with an umbrella, a sparkler, and some fruit floating near the top of the glasses.

The waiter plonked the drinks on the table in front of the now flabbergasted tourists, adding;

"One Whan Afta forra you sir, and one Whan Afta forra you as well. Enjoy your dreenks."

I have no doubt whatsoever that there is *not* a drink called a Whan Afta, but somewhere along the line, the sentence "I'll have one after" meant something to the waiter, and the drink certainly sounded like a 'Whan Afta' when it was introduced to them at the table.

If anyone does happen to know what this drink may be, I would strongly suggest that you don't try it. It's warm for a start, it's like drinking hot perfume, and it could surely be used in aviation as an alternative fuel if there is ever a kerosene shortage.

In fact, it was so bad, the lads only managed about six pints of it!

Easter Sunday – match day

One of the biggest disappointments of the Italy trip was the year when the game fell on Easter Sunday.

The tour party prepared for what should have been the best day of the tour.

Match day arrived, the reason why they were there! Hangovers were shrugged off and, needing the hair of the dog, the party took to the streets of Rome to get a liquid breakfast.

After trying a few bars and cafes and failing to get a drink, it seemed as though the Welsh had drunk the Italians out of alcohol. Wot, no booze?

People started to panic and frustration crept in as kick off approached and still no pre-match beverages seemed to be available.

Then all was revealed – it was Easter Sunday and according to Italian law, no alcohol was to be consumed on that day. So that was it.

Despite the explanation, many people thought this was an excuse and that the Welsh had actually 'drunk them dry'.

Whatever the truth of the matter was, this is the reason that was given 'back home' for a 'dry day' in Rome.

FRANCE

The journey to France, and the options are pretty similar to the Irish trip. Ferries, planes and oh, the Eurotunnel. And you're going in the other direction. Er… it's much more expensive and… er… it takes a lot longer. They talk funny in Ireland, when you arrive, and well… so do the French. They actually talk funnier than the Irish. So funny, that you can't understand the French at all, whereas you can understand the Irish if you put your mind to it.

On second thoughts, it's nothing like the Irish trip at all.

The French can be a little more reserved than other tourists. I think it must be the wine.

Mind you, if you drink enough pints of that stuff, things can get a bit frantic!

The authorities don't seem to be as 'understanding' as the UK law enforcers; they sort of exude this air of 'don't mess about over here mate'.

Of course, there is a lot of 'messing about' going on, but it tends to be more 'in-house' – you know, keep it to ourselves sort of thing.

Head Slap with a Difference

It was in France where one of the most despicable sentences ever issued by a Kangaroo Court was carried out.

One poor soul, who was found guilty of not wearing his dummy in the shower, was given the penalty of two 'gotchas'.

What's this? Something to do with Noel Edmonds? Nobody would say.

In fact three days went by and nothing had happened. Had he got away with it?

He was beginning to think so.

That night was a particularly heavy one, booze-wise. The guilty man went to bed and immediately fell into a deep sleep. He was a heavy sleeper anyway, but the booze just added to his inability to wake up when 'things were happening'.

So, what was happening? His hands were being tied to his 'wedding tackle' – still didn't wake up.

When however, a sharp slap was applied to his forehead, he did wake up!

Now when you're asleep, if someone slaps you on the

forehead, the natural reaction is to throw your arms up and cover your forehead with your hands. If your hands were tied to your 'nether regions' you wouldn't bother would you? But if you didn't know…!

Luckily enough, they were tied with long enough bits of string to make sure that lasting damage wasn't done, but it still gave him a bit of a jolt.

The whole exercise was finished off with a loud rendition of "GOTCHA", from the lads who were crowded around his bed.

And this is the cruel bit. They only administered the one 'Gotcha', but can you imagine the hell he must have gone through while he was waiting for the second one.

Seen my Room?

It was France again, different trip, different year, but another trick involving sleeping arrangements.

One party member got left behind in a bar and returned much later than the rest. He was very very drunk. He went to his room, turned on the light – it was completely empty!

He checked his key, he checked the number on the door – he had the right room. So where was it? He mentioned it to another member of the tour party who casually reported;

"I couldn't swear to it, but I think I saw it on the lawn earlier on."

Confused by this, the 'roomless' tourist staggered out of the hotel to find his room standing alone in the centre of the lawn. It had been stripped piece by piece and re-erected perfectly in a new alfresco setting. Everything was exactly as he'd left it – even the loose Tic-Tacs on his bedside table were in the same place as they were when the table was inside the building.

Tiredness, and booze were beginning to take over now and he could do with a good sleep.

It was a long way to get back into the hotel and climb the stairs to an empty room. Well, his room was here, on the lawn with him – so, off to bed he went.

The next morning, he was in deep trouble – with the hotel manager himself! He woke up to the sound of French being spoken very loudly and quickly and assumed it was a call for breakfast. He got up, got dressed and started to head for the restaurant.

This irritated the manager even more. He ran after our hero and almost manhandled him back to the room. It became obvious from the gestures and body language that he wanted the room taken back into the hotel and replaced in its rightful place. What's more, he was not going to employ any of the hotel staff to help either!

Good job the lads were there to help eh? Well, they were there. They didn't help though.

SCOTLAND

Scotland is a long way from Wales. Ooh, about 6–7 hours on the train, about an hour by plane or nine hours by bus.

So which is the most popular method of transport to Scotland? Well, obviously by bus innit?

Nine hours in a bus is a long time, it must be very boring. Well, there's nothing to do on a bus is there? Is there? You'd be surprised.

The most popular trip involving buses is the flier trip. A flier trip involves driving up in the early hours of the day of the game, and driving back on the same night – usually after the pubs shut in Edinburgh. Here buses make the trip mainly through the hours of darkness. They begin their trek, usually around closing time, by collecting their passengers from pubs along the route. The passengers, already well oiled, will board the bus, armed with luggage, money, and enough booze to last the journey.

"But if they've been in the pub all night, and they get on the bus after 11pm, it won't be long before they drop off to sleep." I hear you say.

No, not really. I suppose there are the odd 'quiet' spells, but on the whole, the inboard entertainment is relentless and not for the softhearted.

As most of the travelling takes place at night, the scope for participation in the fine art of 'mooning' is very restricted due to the lack of motorists around to witness it. Instead, most of the activities are aimed at those who are inside the bus.

Peebles

One thing that became apparent to one group of lads on a flier, was the vicinity of Peebles to everywhere else in Scotland.

They first noticed a road-sign saying 'Peebles six miles' and assumed that they were six miles from Peebles. A fair assumption.

Then they noticed another, and they had certainly travelled more than six miles since they saw the first sign! Then another, then another! And another!

In fact, they decided that wherever they went in Scotland, they were never further than six miles away from Peebles!

Now there must be a rational explanation for this. We know that Scotland isn't circular, having only a six mile radius with Peebles right at the centre of it! So what was going on?

I have narrowed it down to three possibilities, although I have nothing to substantiate any of them;

- Over the last forty years, a rugby club had pinched the same 'Peebles six miles' sign as a kind of 'ritual' every time they'd reached that spot. The Peebles District Council had replaced the sign every time it went missing, only for it to be pinched again by the same rugby club the next time they came across it.

- That particular year, the offending rugby club decided to return *all* the signs, but distribute them all over the Scottish countryside, instead of in their rightful place.

- All the occupants of the bus were so drunk that they couldn't read any of the signs that they saw en route and believed that all signs said the same as the first one they'd seen when they were sober enough to 'take in' what was on it.

  Peebles has a ring-road and the bus driver mistakenly did forty two laps of it without realising that they had been going round in circles for about four hours.

Happy Birthday Dad

Father and son were both going to Scotland for the match – the trouble is, they were going on different trips.

Dad went up for three days with a crowd of friends his age. Son went up on a flier with a crowd of friends his age. Dad was celebrating his birthday in Scotland that year. It was usually celebrated north of the border every two years, and what better place to 'toast another year' than in a country famous for whisky and hospitality.

Mum was keen to get her husband's birthday cards to him so he could open them in Scotland, so she gave them to her son to take up and pass them on.

Son was gobsmacked at the very thought that his mum thought that it was even remotely likely that he'd bump into his dad, but took them anyway.

And you've guessed it already! The first person that son saw when he walked into the first pub in Edinburgh, was his dad! Wow!

"Here you are dad, got your cards for you."

"Cheers son, fancy a pint?"

"Aye, go on then."

As casual as if the encounter had been down the local club!

Fire!

Scotland is a very cold place. Not the people, the climate. Very cold it is, even at the best of times. Still, when you're cwtshed up in a lovely warm hotel or pub, it doesn't really matter what its like outside does it?

Well it does when it's colder *in* the hotel than it is outside.

I know it's not rugby tourists' priority to find five star accommodation; any old 'hole' will do – as long as you can 'get your head down' and have a good greasy breakfast to soak up the booze, it'll do. Of course the cheaper and nastier, the more money will be available to indulge in shenanigans.

Well, one group of trippers actually managed to book into a hotel that appeared to have no form of heating in the place whatsoever. As cheap and nasty goes, this place was certainly the worst they could imagine – and yes, it was colder inside than it was outside.

On the second night, the lads were deep in conversation about what they could do to warm themselves up. One of the suggestions, which they finally decided was the best one after they had considered all the others, was to light a campfire. They could sit around it and snuggle up together and have a sing song. Lovely!!

So after finding some wood, cardboard, paper and anything that would burn they constructed their fire and lit it. They sat down around the fire and looked forward to the first moments when the heat would once again start the circulation going. Er… did I mention that they built and lit the fire on the floor in one of the boys' rooms? No? Well they did. Good job there was no carpet to worry about.

So, there they were, cuddled up together having a marvellous time, and experiencing the feeling of being warm for the first time since getting off the bus that took them up there.

Suddenly, the hotel owner, who had been made aware of the fact that there was a fire in someone's room, not as a result of a smoke alarm but as a result of smoke belching out of the large gap under the door, came bursting in.

He took one look at the scene, put his hand on his hip, tapped his foot and uttered, "Well I've seen some things going on in this hotel involving rugby boys, but this just about takes the biscuit!"

And that was it! He turned on his heels and left. I know many hotel owners who would probably have had more to say about something like that, but he was obviously resigned to the fact that he was not going to expect much more from the clientele that his hotel attracted.

Cabbages

One member of a tour party was getting a bit 'emotional' after a good drink and started to tell his compatriots how he feared he would never be big enough to play the game at a first class level. Okay, he was maintaining his place in the local side, but he would dearly like to play at a higher level, and one day, maybe, even play for his country. It was his dream for all his mates to be travelling up to Murrayfield to see *him* play.

It was then that a typical rugby/booze orientated 'pearl of wisdom' came out. Eat raw cabbages! Yes, that's right, raw cabbages. Apparently, it is a little-known fact that top rugby players have existed for years on diets that have consisted entirely of raw cabbages. Well, and booze, of course.

The next time the 'budding international' was seen, he was wandering around the hotel foyer, refusing calls to go to breakfast, clutching a rather large vegetable of the cabbage variety.

Now come on fellah, you've been on tours before. How could you fall for that? You're not even a rookie. Nevertheless, his desire to make it big in the game completely outweighed the 'common sense' element, and from now on it was cabbages for him.

He stuck to it as well.

At no time for the duration of the tour was he seen without a cabbage and would periodically be seen to take a bite and munch away like a true herbivore.

He did not relish the mastication process of his chosen diet; in fact, from the descriptions I have been given of his facial features when he was doing it, they seemed to be very similar to a face my dog pulled one evening when I dropped a piece of lemon I was slicing in the kitchen – she wolfed it down before it reached the floor.

Just picture that for a moment.

Instead of getting bigger, the cabbage diet made him much slimmer and very unpopular on long coach journeys. Nevertheless, he did achieve success at rugby in later years. Sadly, it seems that this success would have come a lot earlier in his career, if he hadn't gone through his 'green period'.

Aerosol Cans

Picture the scene. A rather more upmarket hostelry than some of the other places mentioned earlier, still, no sign of a star on the hotel's stationery but just the job for some friends to stay whilst on a trip to Scotland for the match.

In the hotel lounge a group of younger members of the tour party had made an interesting discovery. If you hold a lit cigarette lighter in front of an aerosol can and give it a squirt, you get a more than tidy flame thrower! Marvellous!

And what better place to practice technique, and see just how far you can get the flame to go, than the lounge itself?

Unbeknown to them, they were being watched. Not by the hotel staff, but by the hierarchy of the club – you know, the older members. The sensible ones. The pillars of the rugby establishment, those who stand up for the honour of the club, and do everything in their power to maintain the standards which should be observed and adhered to by everyone on tour.

As things started to get a little bit boisterous, the eldest of the elders decided it was time to put a stop to all this tomfoolery. He strode towards the offending group and with a loud bellow pushed out his chest, revealing a newly-acquired symbol of authority in all its glory: his knitted pullover, bearing the club's badge and motto. A sight to be beheld, specially made for senior members on tour to make them stand out from the rest of the party.

After remonstrating with the youngsters for a few moments, reminding them of the duty they have to the club, not to mention the dangers involved in participating in such rash activities, he returned to the other elders at the bar.

Returning with him was his knitted pullover bearing the club's badge and motto. Only this time there was something different about it.

It was sporting a large hole at about 'stomach level', almost perfectly round, exuding from which was a strong smell of burning wool.

The hole was about the size of … er… say about the size of something that had suffered a direct hit from a flame caused by someone holding a lit cigarette lighter in front of an aerosol can and then squirting it.

That told 'em eh?

Off to Scotland Again!

There is a minibus that leaves its village every two years, heading for Scotland. It has done so for a dozen or more years now, but it has never actually gone further than the North West of England. Why is this?

When the trip was first organised, they decided to stop at a place in the North West to stretch their legs, have something to eat and use the toilet facilities.

Also utilizing the same facilities was a minibus containing a group of young ladies, who were en route to another destination, also associated with partying and general 'good times'.

After chatting with their new 'female chums' over motorway service station bacon and eggs, they decided to abandon the Scotland idea and head west to the coast to indulge in a quite different form of entertainment than they had planned. Well, it's nearer isn't it?

Such a good time was had by all, that they decided to reconvene two years later at the same hotel and with the same people.

And so it has gone on ever since.

Presents are not a problem as there are loads of shops that sell things like shortbread biscuits and other Scottishy trinkets that can be given to spouses on their return.

Although, I did hear of one member of the trip who was spotted getting off the bus back home, carrying a large plastic model of Blackpool Tower as his 'offering' and memento of the trip. When the unsuitability of this gift was pointed out, the model was swiftly donated to the local charity shop which was conveniently situated between the bus 'drop off point' and his home.

It's a pity really. It was a lovely model. It lit up and all.

ENGLAND

Because of the closeness of England, geographically speaking, to Wales, it is much more popular to travel there and back on the day of the match.

People can leave on the morning of the match and be back home at a reasonable time the same night – 'rugby special' trains are very popular, cars, minibuses and of course fliers.

People who travel by car do not indulge in the 'festivities' of the occasion as much as those who take trains, minibuses or fliers. Can you imagine what it would be like trying to mirror the activities that go on during the other journeys, when there are just four of you in an Astra? I dare say some have tried, but none have been brought to my attention.

This does not mean that organised 'stay over' trips do not take place in England, and these are just as frenetic as the rest.

English Lessons for the English

One party decided to visit Henley-on-Thames during one of these English sojourns.

The original idea was to take in a bit of English culture and experience the Henley Regatta first hand. The trouble was, this was March, and the regatta wasn't until June. Never mind. Plenty of pubs, let's have a day in Henley and mingle with the locals.

The clientele in Henley-on-Thames pubs are somewhat different to the people that our lads were used to rubbing shoulders with in their locals. These were very 'English'.

Far more 'English' even than those that frequented Twickenham for Wales v England games.

Nevertheless, when the initial shock of such a large influx of loud and uncouth visitors had been overcome, they got on like a house on fire. The language that was used in this pub was quite different. In fact, probably the opposite ends of the evolutionary scale of language, if there is one, was being used that day.

Very little of anything that was said by the Welsh was understood by the English. A little more of the English was understood by the Welsh but there were some massive misinterpretations, one of which is worth mentioning here.

One particularly posh English gent had only popped in for a quick one at lunchtime and enjoyed the bizarre 'goings on' so much that he decided to come back after work to experience the 'Welsh on tour'.

He asked one of the tourists if they would be staying

there for the evening. When told that they would, he told the tourist that he would go straight home from work, take a shower and get into the pub by 6pm at the latest. The trouble is, the English of Henley don't say 'shower' do they? No, they say 'shah'.

The actual conversation went a bit like this;

"Will you be staying in here all day, or will you be moving on?"

"No, we'm in here for the duration like."

"I beg your pardon."

"We'll be in here til we d'get chucked out."

"So you'll be here until closing time tonight?"

"Like I said butt, til we d'get chucked out, which may be closing time, or sooner. Too early to tell see."

"Right, I'll go straight home from the office, have a quick *shah* and hopefully make it back to see you chaps by about six."

"Shah? What sort of shah is that then? You mean… like the shah of Persia or summat?"

This misunderstanding caused a massive bout of hilarity, which developed into an impromptu English pronunciation lesson, where the Welsh boys 'taught' the English how to speak properly, or 'tidy, like' to use the correct phrase.

The pub notice board was used to illustrate the lessons that were learnt. From memory, it was something like this.

It was not long before the notice board was 'wiped' to make way for another impromptu activity. One of the lads had been rummaging through a cleaning cupboard that was situated in a corner between the bar and the toilets and found a long-abandoned dartboard. He dusted it down and strode into the bar with the dartboard held above his head in triumph.

"Let's play darts."

The landlord announced that sadly there were no darts in the pub, darts was not a popular game in these parts.

"Darts? You don't need darts to play darts mun. Oi, stick that board up somewhere, let's 'ave a game is it?"

Our hero 'stuck the board up somewhere' by standing on a chair, holding the dart board as far above his head as he could. Everyone got ready.

When the 'board holder' was fully 'braced' a shout of "Game on" was heard, and less than a second later the air was thick with projectiles coming from every angle of the room.

Everything that would fly was hurled unceremoniously at the dartboard – well, not at the dartboard really, at the poor guy who was holding it up. He stood his ground though, and got a loud cheer from everyone in the pub, including the landlord when he managed to get down off the chair, fully intact and still holding the dartboard.

So that was another game over and done with then.

The whole day was a catalogue of activities of a similar ilk, too many and too near the knuckle to mention here, but the English loved it.

One that is worth a mention, though, is a conversation that developed into something huge.

During a quieter moment, one of the locals was relieving himself in the toilets when he was joined by one of the Welsh lads who also needed to take a leak.

"Who on earth are you lot?"

"Well, we'm all on a trip see."

"I must say you are extremely funny fellows, do you do this for a living?"

"Nah, we'm just out enjoying ourselves mun, you know."

"Where are you from?"

"Wales mun. Do you recognise me?"

"No, are you famous?"

"No, but I just wondered if you noticed the family like-ness."

"Do you have a famous relation?"

"Aye, you know Gareth Edwards? Well, he's my brother."

"Gareth Edwards, the famous Welsh rugby star of the seventies?"

"Aye, that's him. He's my brother he is."

At that point, another of the Welsh boys came into the toilet. He was short and fat with a shock of ginger hair, so striking that it would make a Neil Jenkins wig look bland!

The two, by now deep in conversation, turned to see who had just walked in. In a flash, our hero added, "And see him by there, that's Barry John's brother."

"I say, are you all related to Welsh rugby players?"

"Well that's what the trip is see, butt; we're the 'Brothers of the Seventies Wales Team Association' and we're on a short tour of England, finishing up in Twickers on Saturday for the match."

"Well I must say, this is absolutely fascinating. I can't wait to tell all the chaps in the bar about this."

Too late! Barry John's *brother* had already 'jolly well' gone in the bar and done it. He only told the Welsh lads though. Instantly they were transformed into the brother of some ultra famous rugby player. One actually made a double transfor-mation! After deciding to be Derek Quinnell's brother, he discovered that someone else had already claimed that identity. Instead he became Mary Hopkin's brother, and was invited on the tour in recognition of having spoken to Paul McCartney on the phone.

By the time, the 'true identities' of the strange Welsh visitors had filtered around the bar, the 'brothers' were ready for it.

Of course, they were now even more popular than before. The beer flowed and the landlord organised a free pub lunch for the visitors, who by this time had reached minor celebrity status.

The tales that were told were fantastic. I just wish some of them had been true.

"Aye, I was always a much better kicker than our Barry, the trouble is, I hurt my foot see. Had to teach him to do it instead."

"Merv is a big lad I know, but petrified of spiders he is. I remember our mam coming in one day and said there was a big 'un in the bath. Well, our Merv was gone! Shifted faster that he ever has on the pitch!"

"They d'call our John 'JPR'. That's because of the other John Williams in the side see. Stops confusion. They call him JJ. His brother isn't here today. He's only got a sister see. Girls are not allowed on this trip. Well anyway, our John's favourite football team is QPR. The name is so similar see…"

And so on.

At the end of the night the English were very sorry to see their new friends leaving. Many of the lads left with addresses written on beer mats and fag packets to honour promises to send autographs and other memorabilia concerning their famous brothers to their English fans.

Of course, nothing ever arrived in the Henley-on-Thames area. Well nothing to do with rugby anyway. More to do with Representative from Encyclopaedia Britannica, free samples, memberships to book clubs, video clubs and just about anything that is advertised in Sunday supplements: "View for seven days absolutely FREE. Just send your address to…"

The 'Brothers of the Seventies Wales Team Association' indeed!

I'll have a '99' Please

Another impromptu moment, this time on another tour, was the theft on an ice-cream van. A group of lads were taking a well-deserved break from the usual festivities associated with a rugby trip. It was a lovely day and there was a nice little park visible from the hotel window. It would be lovely to take a little stroll around there – you know, get a bit of fresh air, clear the head a bit.

It was such a lovely day, that there was an ice-cream van parked by the lake, doing a roaring trade – and this was in February!

After a few laps of the park, they sat on the grass near the ice-cream van to watch the people who were congregating around it: particularly at some 'tasty' looking young ladies, who were tucking into some very inviting-looking 99s.

Just as one of the lads asked if anyone fancied an ice-cream, another sharp-eyed member of the group noticed the van owner locking the vehicle up and heading off in the direction of the park's conveniences.

"Why have an ice-cream when we can have the whole van?"

And before you could say 'Phil Bennett's brother', he was in through the hatch and chugging down the little tarmac path that ran alongside the lake.

It was not long before he decided to park up and sell a few

ice-creams; well, why not, eh? There's no point in having an ice-cream van and not selling any, is there?

He'd not sold that many before the out-of-breath real owner of the van caught up with him. After a lot of shouting and bawling, the hijacker vacated the vehicle and everyone was happy – especially the rest of the lads who had watched the whole episode in awe and disbelief.

If there is a moral to the story, it must be: if you are going to steal an ice-cream van, make sure you know where all the exits are before you do so. Try to remember that little tarmac paths that run alongside lakes usually just follow the perimeter, and if you do not get off and go in another direction, you will end up in the same place that you started from. If you are going to stick to the tarmac path, try to remember that ice-cream vans are very conspicuous. They are designed to be bright and to attract attention, making it easy for owners to spot. Turning the jingle on will also help the owner find you, even if you have managed to park up in a difficult-to-spot place.

Hazardous Driving Conditions

English motorists who were trying to negotiate a busy rounda-bout got more than they bargained for on the day some Welsh tourists commandeered it for use as a punishment for someone who had been found guilty at a Kangaroo Court.

The offender had been tried, found guilty and sentenced to run naked around the busiest roundabout in the vicinity. So this is the sight that greeted vehicles approaching the rounda-bout. But it was nothing compared to what was to come.

The coach had got a funny feeling that something was up and decided to have a look around to check. He was immediately attracted to the sound of shouting, whooping and general hilarity and decided to investigate by heading in the direction that the noise was coming from. He was not a happy chappie when he saw what was going on, and began to lecture them on the ethics of the club, the good name of rugby that was being tarnished and the extremely cruel nature of the punishment that they had doled out. In addition, he felt that they too should face a penalty for these misdemeanors, and ordered the rest of the party to join him!

The motorists who were trying to negotiate the roundabout this time were faced with an even greater hazard compared to the one that had been experienced earlier – the sight of nineteen naked men calmly jogging around it.

Sure enough, the lads became aware that a police car was approaching and would shortly be negotiating *their* roundabout. The siren told them that. The same siren also heralded the departure of the coach, which was nowhere to be seen when the police car arrived. They didn't have much to say: "Boys, you've got two minutes to get dressed and make yourselves scarce."

The scrabble to get to the pile of clothes was something to be witnessed. Sure enough, by the time the two minutes had elapsed, they were all dressed and walking off into the distance. I don't think that any of them were actually dressed in the same clothes that they had on *before* the incident though!

Here Kitty Kitty

Picture the scene: it's very late. It's in the bar of an English hotel and the guy in charge of the beer kitty is so 'refreshed' that he is drifting in and out of consciousness.

During one of his sentient moments, he decided that he

had to do something with the kitty as he was very close to passing out for good.

"Better put it somewhere safe."

So he put it somewhere safe and sure enough, very soon after, he did pass out for good.

Well, not for good, but certainly until the next morning. He came back into the bar, which was used to serve breakfast in the morning, and began to try to remember where he'd put the kitty money. At first, he wasn't too bothered as he was sure that soon something would spur his memory – but nothing did.

He started to hunt around the room without making too much of a fuss about it. He didn't really want to let the rest of the lads know he'd lost the beer money.

"Where is it? Where could I have put it? It *must* be here! If someone on the hotel staff found £1500 in cash, they'd hand it in, wouldn't they?" Would they? WOULD YOU?

Finally he had to tell the lads. Now the whole party is searching for it!

All except for one member of the party. The oldest member in the club. He wasn't out on the pop the night before and knew nothing of the panic that was dominating the breakfast proceedings. Didn't care either.

"Cornflakes would be nice," he thought as he looked around the room to see if he could spot a table that wasn't being turned upside down and examined by the rest of his party.

"Ah, there's one."

Armed with some milk and a box of cornflakes, he made his way to the table and proceeded to pour £1500 cash into his bowl. Hmmm.

And the moral is: if you are staying in a hotel and the bar doubles up as a breakfast room and you want to hide lots of cash, and you decide that a good hiding place would be a breakfast-associated container, make sure you don't opt for the toaster. They may be cold in the night, but they don't half get hot in the morning!

And Finally – The Fans' Greatest Win. Or was it?

Have a look at this headline and see if you can think where it may have come from.

"CHEEKY Welsh rugby fans could scupper plans to name part of the new Wembley Stadium development after one of the great icons in English soccer. "

On 18th February 2005 I received an email from a friend, alerting me to a website that invited people to email suggestions for a name for a new footbridge that was to be built near the new Wembley stadium. The London Development Agency (LDA) had set up a poll to name the bridge after one of Wembley's greatest sporting moments.

The prize was a signed England football shirt, to be awarded to the person who had voted for the name finally chosen.

The email that I received suggested that all Welsh people should enter the competition and put forward the name 'Pont Scott Gibbs', in recognition of the famous winning try against England at Wembley in 1999.

I thought it was a marvellous idea, and, after forwarding the email to all the Welsh people who would be inclined to join in, entered my suggestion of 'Pont Scott Gibbs' into the competition.

I forgot about it after that, then, right out of the blue, I received another email on 30th March 2005 with some good and bad news. It was headed 'Wales Hijack Wembley Bridge' and went on to report that the poll results had revealed that the most popular offering was not Geoff Hurst, Alf Ramsey or Bobby Moore leading the running – but Scott Gibbs!

The LDA confirmed that it had been overwhelmed with responses by Wales fans wanting the bridge named after Gibbs and added that they were adamant that whatever the outcome of the poll, the bridge would NOT be called the 'Scott Gibbs Bridge':

> Officials said they prefer an English football name or moment, although they did confirm more votes have come in for the former Wales centre than any other star or moment in the stadium's history.

"Gibbs is leading the way," admitted an embarrassed officer of the LDA. He played down the significance Gibbs' poll-leading position and insisted, "It's just a bit of fun: you start sending emails and everyone jumps on the bandwagon – this competition is about helping to raise the profile, not just of Wembley but of the whole area."

"The bridge is part of a multi-million pound development of the new Wembley Stadium and its officials were hoping to name it after Sir Alf, Hurst, or the 1966 England World Cup win."

"Everyone is entering a draw for a signed England shirt – and I have to say we have had a few choice comments from Welsh rugby fans on what they would do with it if they won!"

LDA officials have described it as an 'orchestrated campaign' by rugby supporters to name the bridge after Gibbs. His try at Wembley summed him up, the determination to make the line, the pumping legs and the iron-fisted hand-off. He will always be remembered for scoring THAT try, but his abilities made him one of the world's great centres in history. For Wales' legions of rugby fans, the try is the most memorable moment in the stadium's history.

Peter Rogers was prop in the side that beat England. He said it would be fitting to name the bridge after his old team-mate.

"That would be fantastic," he said. "If it is true that most of the suggestions are coming from Welsh rugby supporters that would be great. If people are suggesting Scott's name, then they are the ones with most passion and they should have their votes. I had just come off when Scott scored and I was thinking we'd done well to get that far, within scoring distance of the English."

"It was a great achievement because we were massive underdogs and I was thinking we had done well just to stick with them. When Scott scored the try it was amazing. It happened so quickly and was apparently from an unplanned move. When he went over the line it was fantastic, and we had only just beaten France."

"There was a lot of spirit and we were like a big family at one stage. It was just a great day."

Rogers remembers that passion which has hoisted Gibbs to the top of the LDA's poll well.

"Wembley was like a sea of red," he said. "We couldn't believe it, because this was in London of all places. Walking into the stadium, your first thoughts were of all the great footballers and the cup finals held there, but when we went out for the warm-up and Max Boyce and Tom Jones were there singing, that was amazing."

So, did the Welsh suggestion win or didn't it? According to officials, 'Scott Gibbs' was the most popular name offered in the poll. C'mon LDA, '*chwarae teg*, do the decent thing and give the bridge its deserved name,' I heard ringing around the valleys as the result was imminent.

They named it the White Horse Bridge – well, it was only fair I suppose, wasn't it?

I hear that Newport City Council are planning a new bridge to span the river Usk, due for completion in May 2006. Newport Rugby Club are campaigning to have it named after prominent stars that have graced Rodney Parade over the years.

Let's hope they keep the campaign a bit low key and keep it in-house, as it were. I mean, we don't want anyone to be tempted to sabotage a poll and leave Newport City Council-lors having to ponder the thought of cutting the tape followed by the words, "And I name this bridge the Johnny Wilkinson Bridge."

Perish the thought!

Welsh
Valleys
Characters

David
Jandrell

Welcome to the world of the Welsh valleys characters. Enjoy this delightful introduction to these real characters – their hants, habits and humour.

£3.95 ISBN: 0 86243 772 5

Welsh
Rugby
Heroes

Androw
Bennett

£3.95 ISBN: 0 86243 772 5

Welsh Valleys Humour

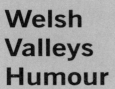

David Jandrell

A first-time visitor to the south Wales Valleys will be subjected to a language that will initially be unfamiliar to them. This book features a tongue-in-cheek guide to the curious ways in which Valleys inhabitants use English, together with anecdotes, jokes, stories depicting Valleys life, and malapropisms from real-life Valleys situations!

"What a delight David Jandrell's book is!"
– **Ronnie Barker**

£3.95

ISBN: 0 86243 736 9

Welsh Rugby Stories is just one
of a whole range of Welsh-interest
publications from Y Lolfa. For a full list
of books currently in print, send now
for your free copy of our new, full colour
catalogue. Or simply surf into our website

www.ylolfa.com

for secure on-line ordering.

TALYBONT CEREDIGION CYMRU SY24 5AP
e-bost ylolfa@ylolfa.com
gwefan www.ylolfa.com
ffôn (01970) 832 304
ffacs 832 782